MAKE A JOYFUL NOISE

McDougal & Associates
Servants of Christ and Stewards of the Mysteries of God

MAKE A JOYFUL NOISE

An Introduction to Praise and Worship

by

Prophetess Jackie Harewood

Unless otherwise noted, all Scripture quotations are from *The Holy Bible, Authorized King James Version,* public domain.

MAKE A JOYFUL NOISE
Copyright © 2018—Jacqueline Harewood
ALL RIGHTS RESERVED
No part of this book may be reproduced or transmitted in any form or by any means, electronic or mechanical, including photocopying, recording, or by any information retrieval system.

Published by:

McDougal & Associates
18896 Greenwell Springs RD
Greenwell Springs, LA 70739
www.thepublishedword.com

McDougal & Associates is dedicated to the spreading of the Gospel of Jesus Christ to as many people as possible
in the shortest time possible.

ISBN 978-1-940461-74-8

Printed in the US, the UK and Australia
For Worldwide Distribution

DEDICATION

This book is dedicated to my many denominational friends who could never understand why it took all that to praise God. I pray that this book will give you revelation into the joy of praise and worship.

ACKNOWLEDGEMENTS

My thanks to my husband, Apostle David Harewood, for having patience with me for having taken on yet another challenge, which decreases the amount of time we can spend together. Thanks for sharing my happiness when starting this book and following with encouragement when it seemed too difficult to be completed. I would probably have given up without your support.

CONTENTS

Introduction 9

What Is Praise? 13
The Power of Praise 14
The Power of Individual Praise 16
The Benefits of Praise 20
Understanding Our Responses 23
Purely Mechanical Praise 32
The Basics of True Praise and Worship 34
A Comparison of Praise and Worship 38
Praise in the Old Testament 41
Worship in the Wilderness Tabernacle 45
The Functions of Praise and Worship 50
What Are Spiritual Sacrifices? 52
What Is "an Acceptable Sacrifice"? 54
What Are the Effects of an Acceptable
    Sacrifice 57
What Are Spiritual Songs? 59
Hindrances to Praise and Worship 61
Five Types of Praise 63
Congregational Praise 64

The Power of Praise in Prayer.................... 67
Praise as a Weapon... 70
Three Powerful Weapons 72
Launching Rockets with Warheads 74
Reasons We Don't Enter In 76
The Correct Approach to Praise 79
What Are the High Praises of God?............ 81
Praise as Warfare 84
Clapping as a Powerful Form of Warfare.. 90
Worship Like the Royal Priesthood You Are 95
Standards for Our Worship 97
In Conclusion 101

Other Books by Jackie Harewood............. 106

Author Contact Page 113

INTRODUCTION

Early in my Christian life and ministry, I realized the power that lies in praise and worship. When God said to His people, ***"Make a joyful noise unto the Lord,"*** He was not just desiring our adoration. He knew that praise and worship could become a powerful weapon of intercession in our hands to be used against the enemy of our souls.

True, we must praise God for who He is and for what He does. He is worthy of all praise. Then, we must go beyond praise, into the intimate atmosphere of worship, to commune with the Creator one-on-one and receive from His hand. But our praise and worship mean much more than that.

Over the years, I have done many teaching on this all-important subject, in an attempt to equip God's little ones with the weapons they need and cause them to rise up and become effective soldiers in God's Kingdom.

What follows is a compilation of many of those teachings. They have already changed countless lives, and I know they will change your life too. Get ready to *Make A Joyful Noise*.

Prophetess Jackie Harewood
Baton Rouge, Louisiana

Psalm 98:1

O sing unto the Lord a new song. For he hath done marvellous things; his right hand, and his holy arm, hath gotten him the victory

Verse 4

Make a joyful noise unto the Lord, all the earth; make a loud noise, and rejoice, and sing praise.

Verse 5

Sing unto the Lord with the harp; with the harp, and the voice of a psalm.

Make a joyful noise unto the LORD, all ye lands.

Serve the LORD with gladness: come before his presence with singing.

Know ye that the LORD he is God: it is he that hath made us, and not we ourselves; we are his people, and the sheep of his pasture.

Enter into his gates with thanksgiving, and into his courts with praise: be thankful unto him, and bless his name.

For the LORD is good; his mercy is everlasting; and his truth endureth to all generations.

Psalm 100

WHAT IS PRAISE?

Praise is an act of your will.

¹ I will extol thee, my God, O king; and I will bless thy name for ever and ever.
² Every day will I bless thee; and I will praise thy name for ever and ever.
⁶ I will declare thy greatness.
⁷ I will speak of the glorious honor of thy majesty, and of thy wondrous works.

Psalm 145

THE POWER OF PRAISE

I. **Praise is not a mass function; it is a response of an individual to God.**

II. **The purpose of praise**

1. Praise gets God on the scene.

But thou art holy, O thou that inhabitest the praises of Israel. Psalm 22:3

2. Praise establishes a closer and more intimate Relationship with God.

THE POWER OF PRAISE

3. Praise keeps you focused, keeps you from going under.

   A. Peter went under when he took his eyes off of Jesus. When he saw the boisterous winds, he was afraid and began to sink (see Matthew 14:30)

III. When you talk or sing about Jesus and what He has done, excitement and anticipation begin to build in your spirit.

THE POWER OF INDIVIDUAL PRAISE

I. In our daily lives:

1. Army troops find it is easier if they sing while marching. Singing helps them not to think about the weight of their backpacks or the distance they must still travel. Their focus is tuned to the rhythm of the song, and consequently their steps seem lighter. As they pick up the cadence of the beat, before they know it, they have finished the course.

THE POWER OF INDIVIDUAL PRAISE

I have fought a good fight, I have finished my course, I have kept the faith. 2 Timothy 4:7

Praise is vital to our daily lives. It allows us to rise above circumstances, doubts and fears. It allows us to rise higher so that we can get a fresh perspective through God's viewpoint.

A. Natural giants opposed the children of Israel, but Caleb saw through God's eyes (see Numbers 13:17, 28 and 30).

B. Spiritual giants continually try to oppose us today.

We wrestle not against flesh and blood. Ephesians 6:12

   C. Those giants are already defeated.

And having spoiled principalities and powers, he made a show of them openly, triumphing over them in it. Colossians 2:15

   D. We can use Joshua 6:1-5 as a model for our spiritual Jerichos.

      1. We compass our difficulties with the Word.

      2. We can then sing praises.

THE POWER OF INDIVIDUAL PRAISE

3. As you spend time in praise, you will find that your cares and disappointments will disappear.

4. Praise should become a way of life.

My heart is fixed, O God, my heart is fixed: I will sing and give praise. Awake up, my glory; awake, psaltery and harp: I myself will awake early. Psalm 57:7

THE BENEFITS OF PRAISE

1. Praise increases your faith, and, as you sing about the benefits of God, even your attitude changes.

2. As you enter into praise, you tap a hidden reservoir of God's power.

3. Praise increases your strength.

The joy of the Lord is your strength.
Nehemiah 8:10

Praise is what ushers you into joy.

THE BENEFITS OF PRAISE

4. Praise brings encouragement to your spirit.

5. Praise changes the spiritual attitude of a home.

6. Praise refreshes you physically.

   ... The garment of praise for the spirit of heaviness... Isaiah 61:3

7. Praise lifts our spirits since expressing our confidence in God through praise will bring us peace in the midst of any storm.

8. Praise brings increase.

   Then shall the earth yield her increase. Psalm 67:6

MAKE A JOYFUL NOISE

Note: You cannot manipulate God, but if your praise of Him is from the heart, it will move Him.

UNDERSTANDING OUR RESPONSES

I present two figures on the following pages. Figure 1 represents you, the praiser. Figure 2 also represent you, your inner person who controls all of your attitudes, desires and impulses. This is your soul, which is comprised of your intellect, your emotions and your will.

1. During praise, Figure 1 may rise to the occasion, sing, dance and even shout and yet, not one iota of worship may result.

FIGURE 1

FIGURE 2

2. Your inner person (Figure 2) may be gritting its teeth and saying, "I don't feel like praising God."

You (Figure 1) continue to sing, raising your hands in praise, while your inner man (Figure 2) remains bowed over, depressed or even in rebellion.

You must have unity in the various parts of your person.

The body, the soul and the spirit must be in agreement. If not, you will not and you cannot move into worship!

UNDERSTANDING OUR RESPONSES

Jesus said unto him, thou shalt love the lord thy god with all thy soul and with all thy mind.
                    Matthew 22:37

You must learn to love the Lord with your emotions:

The heart is all your inward affections.

The soul is all your consciousness

The mind is all your thoughts.

1. A house divided against itself cannot stand (see Mark 3:25).

2. How can two walk together except they agree (see Amos 3:3).

MAKE A JOYFUL NOISE

For we know that if our earthly house of this tabernacle were dissolved, we have a building of god, a house not made with hands, eternal in the heavens. 2 Corinthians 5:1

Our body is considered to be a house. Our soul, our body and our spirit must be united.

Every city or house divided against itself shall not stand.
                               Matthew 12:25

Worship is a personal response.

The song "Set My Spirit Free that I Might Worship Thee" expresses what we are desiring to achieve.

UNDERSTANDING OUR RESPONSES

Singing is meant to lead to praise. It affords expression for our emotions.

Praise can then move you into worship.

Praise is commanded by God, but worship is a response which cannot be commanded.

In Psalm 42:5, David cried out, *"Why art thou cast down, O my soul?"* He was talking to his inner man (Figure 2), his soul—his intellect, will and emotions. David realized that the body and soul must line up. At that moment, his spirit did not feel like worshipping. It was under the control of his soul.

God did not design the Christian life to be lived under the domination of the soul, where emotions, intellect, and double-mindedness can rule. He desires that we discipline ourselves to be ruled by our spirit in an attitude of constant communion with Him.

THE SOUL VS. THE SPIRIT

Mary, the mother of Jesus, said:

A. *"My soul doth magnify the Lord."*

B. *"And my spirit hath rejoiced in God my Savior"* (Luke 1:46-47).

In this, we see the dual relationship between soul and spirit in praise and worship.

UNDERSTANDING OUR RESPONSES

A. With her understanding, Mary magnified the Lord, and with her will, emotions and intellect, she considered God's greatness.

B. When she moved in harmony toward praise, she then proceeded to worship, as her spirit rejoiced in the Lord.

PURELY MECHANICAL PRAISE

Beware of mechanical praise:

1. **Don't just perform songs**

    A. Songs should reflect our praise and adoration of God.

    B. Songs should draw our attention to God.

2. **Don't just keep time to the beat.**

PURELY MECHANICAL PRAISE

Some music just appeals to our emotions, not our spirit. Be careful of the beat! Music that appeals to the natural person can hinder worship.

4. Much singing is not really praise.

   A. A genuine praise must flow from the heart of an individual to God.

   B. Singing from the depths of our heart out of gratitude is true praise.

Beware of **PROGRAMS** and **SCHEDULES**.

THE BASICS OF TRUE PRAISE AND WORSHIP

1. Come before the Lord with thanksgiving and praise.

2. Come with an attitude of gratitude, bringing with you the sacrifice of praise.

3. Seek to follow the leading of the Holy Spirit.

THE BASICS OF TRUE PRAISE AND WORSHIP

4. Expect to make and effort to participate with the Holy Spirit's leading. He is the One directing your praise and worship.

5. Learn to press past condemnation.
There is therefore now no condemnation to them which are in Christ Jesus, who walk not after the flesh, but after the spirit. Romans 8:1

6. Expect, with some effort and struggle, for praise to turn into worship.

Casting down imaginations, and every high thing that exalteth itself against the knowledge of God, and bringing into captivity every thought to the obedience of Christ." 2 Corinthians 10:5

MAKE A JOYFUL NOISE

God looks at our heart. He knows our real priorities, the real object of our worship and affection, our excitement (or lack of excitement), our wonder (or lack of wonder), and our desire (or lack of desire).

He is a jealous God who wants to be the the focus of our affection (see Psalm 139:1-3). He is the Creator of all things, the God who spoke humankind into existence, and He wants you to worship Him.

Many people know God, but not many actually enjoy being in His presence.

1. Praise builds up our spirits (see 1 Corinthians 14 and Jude 20).

THE BASICS OF TRUE PRAISE AND WORSHIP

2. Therefore praise should be our continual sacrifice to God, the fruit of our lips (see Hebrews 13:15).

A COMPARISON OF PRAISE AND WORSHIP

Praise	Worship
Lifting hands	Kissing God's hand
Rejoicing	Reverence
Blessing	Obeisance
Adoration	Awe
Celebrating (foolishly)	Laying prostrate
	Bowing
	Stooping

A COMPARISON OF PRAISE AND WORSHIP

Boasting	Paying homage
Thanksgiving	Devotion
Making music in the Spirit	Lifting voices in the Spirit

Praise blesses the heart of God, and God delights in the praise of His people.

God dwells and manifests His power where His people are lifting up their voices to praise to him.

> A. When David had returned the Ark of the Covenant to Jerusalem, he set up a tent to house it and appointed four thousand priests to stand before it, play their

instruments and praise the Lord (see 1 Chronicles 23:5 and 30).

B. Levites were appointed as ministers before the Ark of the Lord, to celebrate and to thank and praise the God of Israel (1 Chronicles 16:6).

Praise is done in holiness (see Psalm 29:2).

Praise precedes worship.

PRAISE IN THE OLD TESTAMENT

1. Who or what was to be praised?

Psalm 140

God, their king (see verse 2)

God's name (see verse 3)

2. From where were the praises to originate?

Psalm 148

From Heaven (see verses 1-6)

From the Earth (see verses 7-12)

From God's sanctuary (see Psalm 150:1)

3. Who was to praise God?

Psalm 148

His people (see verse 13)

4. How are we to praise?

Psalm 150

With the sound of trumpets, psalteries and harps (see verse 3)

PRAISE IN THE OLD TESTAMENT

With the timbrel and dance, and with string instruments and organs (see verse 4)

With loud cymbals and high-sounding cymbals (see verse 5)

With their mouths (see verse 6)

Let everything that hath breath praise the LORD. *Praise ye the* LORD. Psalm 150:6

5. How were they to approach God?

Psalm 100:1-5
With a joyful noise (see verse 1)
With gladness and singing (see verse 2)

With thanksgiving (see verse 3)

6. Where were they to Worship?

In the courts of the Tabernacle (see Psalm 100)

As you personally enter into the Holy of Holies before God today, worship takes place.

WORSHIP IN THE WILDERNESS TABERNACLE

I. Entry into the Outer Court represented thanksgiving.

II. Entry into the Holy Place represented praise.

III. Entry into the Holy of Holies represented worship (see Psalm 110).

MAKE A JOYFUL NOISE

THE OUTER COURT

Enter into his gates with thanksgiving. Psalm 100:4

1. Thanksgiving is for what God has done.

2. As we prepare to enter the Holy of Holies, we began to recount what the Lord has done.

   A. This involves much action of the body.

   B. It involves the raising of the hands.

   C. It involves clapping of the hands, singing or praising in a loud voice, excitement and the exuberance that marks the beginning of our approach to the Lord.

THE HOLY PLACE – PRAISE

I. Praise is a function of the will (represented by the showbread).

1. We submit our will to God.

    A. We sing songs of submission:

    1. In My Life, Be Glorified

    2. Lord, I Want to Be More Like You

3\. I Need Thee Every Hour

II. The candlestick represents the Holy Spirit.

1. We sing in the Spirit and in the understanding (see 1 Corinthians 14:15).

2. We sanctify our minds through the power of the Spirit by singing in the Spirit.

3. Then our emotions take over, bringing us through the veil and into the presence of God in worship.

When we come to that final act of worship, it is the divine invitation of the Lord that draws us within the veil on into God's presence.

1. No individual can program himself for worship.

    A. It is an act of our will to thank God.

    B. It is an act of our will to praise God.

    C. It is an act of God's will to invite us into His presence in the act of worship.

THE FUNCTIONS OF PRAISE AND WORSHIP

Praise deals with the works of God

A. Psalm 100

B. Psalm 103

C. Psalm 104

D. Psalm 111

THE FUNCTIONS OF PRAISE AND WORSHIP

Worship deals with the personhood of God

A. Psalm 29:2, 45:11 and 95:6

B. Isaiah 6

C. Acts 9

D. Revelation 4

WHAT ARE SPIRITUAL SACRIFICES?

Ye also, as lively stones, are built up a spiritual house, an holy priesthood, to offer up spiritual sacrifices, acceptable to God by Jesus Christ.
1 Peter 2:5

I. Offer yourself.

I beseech you therefore, brethren, by the mercies of God, that ye present your bodies a living sacrifice, holy,

WHAT ARE SPIRITUAL SACRIFICES?

acceptable unto God, which is your reasonable service. Romans 12:1

II. Offer praise.

By him therefore let us offer the sacrifice of praise to God continually, that is, the fruit of our lips giving thanks to his name.

Hebrews 13:15

III. Do good and fellowship with one another.

But to do good and to communicate forget not: for with such sacrifices God is well pleased.

Hebrews 13:16

WHAT IS "AN ACCEPTABLE SACRIFICE"?

Here are some characteristics of an acceptable sacrifice:

1. Honesty

But the hour cometh, and now is, when the true worshippers shall worship the Father in spirit and in truth: for the Father seeketh such to worship him. John 4:23

WHAT IS "AN ACCEPTABLE SACRIFICE"?

2. In the Spirit

For we are the circumcision, which worship God in the spirit, and rejoice in Christ Jesus, and have no confidence in the flesh.
Philippians 3:3

3. Gratitude and reverence

Wherefore we receiving a kingdom which cannot be moved, let us have grace, whereby we may serve God acceptably with reverence and godly fear. Hebrews 12:28

4. Faith

By faith Abel offered unto God a more excellent sacrifice than Cain, by which he obtained witness that he was righteous, God testifying of his gifts: and by it he being dead yet speaketh. Hebrews 11:4

5. Righteousness

And he shall sit as a refiner and purifier of silver: and he shall purify the sons of Levi, and purge them as gold and silver, that they may offer unto the Lord an offering in righteousness. Malachi 3:3

WHAT ARE THE EFFECTS OF AN ACCEPTABLE SACRIFICE?

1. We have the glory of God and His presence in our midst (see 2 Chronicles 5 and 7).

2. We gain power over our enemies (see 2 Chronicles 20:21-22).

3. We have financial provision (see 2 Chronicles 1:7 and Isaiah 61:6).

4. We enjoy deliverance from impossible situations (see Jonah 2).

5. Miracles happen in our lives (see Acts 16:25-30).

6. There is a release of spiritual gifts and ministries to us (see Romans 12:1 and 6-8).

7. Church growth is realized (see Acts 2:46-47 and 13:2).

WHAT ARE SPIRITUAL SONGS?

I will sing with the spirit, and I will sing with the understanding also.
                    1 Corinthians 14:15

1. When we sing in tongues, we don't worry about rhyme our words. We are expressing deep feelings in the Spirit. When those moments come, the Spirit of prophecy can come upon us as well, and we can pray with

our understanding the words that we have prayed in the Spirit. These are spiritual songs, words of special ministry to us from the Lord.

2. Praise has a tremendous ability to change attitudes and emotions.

Can you imagine watching a TV program with the music turned off? The sense of ebb and flow, of tension is created by the music. Music has the ability to mold and shape thoughts. It is important to sing under the direction of the Holy Spirit.

HINDRANCES TO PRAISE AND WORSHIP

There are many things that can hinder your ability to praise and worship God. Here are two very big ones, perhaps the biggest ones.

I. Pride (see James 4:6 and 10)

> *What to do:* Humble yourself and make a quality decision to bless God whatever the cost to your pride.

II. Religious Tradition

What to do: Obey.

Serving the Lord with all humility of mind. Acts 20:19

FIVE TYPES OF PRAISE

I. As an individual

II. As a testimonial

III. Corporate praise

IV. Congregational praise

V. Praise with hymns and spiritual songs

CONGREGATIONAL PRAISE

I. Jesus is quoted in Hebrews 2:9-13 concerning congregational praise:

But we see Jesus, who was made a little lower than the angels for the suffering of death, crowned with glory and honour; that he by the grace of God should taste death for every man. For it became him, for whom are all things, and by whom are all things, in bringing many sons unto glory, to make the captain of their salvation perfect through

CONGREGATIONAL PRAISE

sufferings. For both he that sanctifieth and they who are sanctified are all of one: for which cause he is not ashamed to call them brethren, Saying, I will declare thy name unto my brethren, in the midst of the church will I sing praise unto thee. And again, I will put my trust in him. And again, Behold I and the children which God hath given me.

II. Our congregational praise services should reflect our deep reverence for God as a body. It is a command:

Praise ye the Lord. *Sing unto the* Lord *a new song, and his praise in the congregation of saints.*
Psalm 149:1

MAKE A JOYFUL NOISE

Never underestimate the importance of corporate praise and worship. Corporate worship involves the power of agreement, the power of coming into unity. Therefore, during corporate praise, a great spiritual energy is generated.

THE POWER OF PRAISE IN PRAYER

And when her masters saw that the hope of their gains was gone, they caught Paul and Silas, and drew them into the marketplace unto the rulers, and brought them to the magistrates, saying, These men, being Jews, do exceedingly trouble our city, and teach customs, which are not lawful for us to receive, neither to observe, being Romans. And the multitude rose up together against them: and the magistrates rent off their clothes, and commanded to beat them. Acts 16:19-22

I. The action

Paul and Silas were brought before the magistrates (verse 20).

They were accused of teaching customs which were not lawful (verse 21).

The multitude rose up against them (verse 22).

    1. They rent their clothes.

    2. They beat them.

THE POWER OF PRAISE IN PRAYER

II. The reaction

Paul and Silas prayed and sang praises to God (see verse 25).

III. The results

An earthquake came, and the foundations of the prison were shaken (see verse 26).

1. All the doors were opened.

2. Everyone's hands were loosed.

PRAISE AS A WEAPON

I. Praise is a delivery system for the Scriptures.

    A. Internally to your spirit

    B. Externally to attack the enemy

II. Many praise songs are taken from the Bible.

III. Praise is a powerful way to help you proclaim the Scriptures (the memorized Word).

PRAISE AS A WEAPON

IV. Praise is an effective tool at your disposal to oppose the works of the enemy.

V. Music is a powerful medium. Once it is inside your mind, it stays there.

Example:
Studies show that after twenty years people can still remember a great percentage of the words to secular songs they learned in their youth.

THREE POWERFUL WEAPONS

I. The Word, the thoughts of God

II. The name of Jesus (see Acts 3:6, 16, 4:7, 10 and 12)

III. The blood of Jesus (see Revelation 12:11)

HOW TO LAUNCH ROCKETS CARRYING OUR WEAPONS

1. Through prayer

THREE POWERFUL WEAPONS

2. Through preaching

3. Through our testimony

4. Through our praise

5. Through our worship

Praise is our most effective tool, our greatest weapon.

LAUNCHING ROCKETS WITH WARHEADS

1. Rockets can carry a warhead.

2. The power for an explosion and the resulting destruction is in the warhead.

3. The rocket is simply the vehicle which carries the warhead to its intended target.

LAUNCHING ROCKETS WITH WARHEADS

4. God's power for spiritual warfare is in the Word, the name of Jesus and the blood of Jesus.

5. Some rockets that can launch these powerful weapons are:

    1. Prayer

    2. Praise and worship

    3. Preaching

    4. Your testimony

Rockets have no power in themselves, but they carry the power of the warhead to the desired target.

REASONS WE DO NOT ENTER IN

1. We use the wrong approach.

The Solution:

A. Jesus' death resulted in the veil of the Temple being rent (see Matthew 27:51).

B. We can come boldly and enter in by the blood of Jesus (see Hebrews 10:19-22).

REASONS WE DO NOT ENTER IN

2. **Our feelings keep us away.**

   The Solution:
   A. Praise is a decision.

   B. Praise must be an act of our will (see Psalm 145).

3. **We have a sense of unworthiness.**

   The Solution:
   A. The blood of Jesus has forever dealt with sin, guilt and unworthiness.

So Christ was once offered to bear the sins of many; and unto them that look for him shall he appear the second time without sin unto salvation. Hebrews 9:28

B. You have right standing with God regardless of your self-evaluation (see Romans 8:1).

C. The blood of Jesus is over your family and your house and causes judgment to pass over you so that the destroyer cannot come near (see Hebrews 10:22).

D. Your heart has been *"sprinkled"* to cleanse you from a guilty conscience.

E. You overcome by the blood of the Lamb (see Revelation 12:11).

THE CORRECT APPROACH TO PRAISE

I will praise thee with my whole heart: before the gods will I sing praise unto thee. Psalm 138:1

Much depends on the attitude of the heart.

If I regard iniquity in my heart, the Lord will not hear me.
Psalm 66:18

I. We must prepare our hearts before we seek Him."

II. We must be honest with God.

   1. Hebrews 4:16 invites us to *"come boldly."*

   2. Psalm 62:8 invites us: *"pour out your heart before him."*

   3. Psalm 100:4-5 gives us an open invitation to *"enter."*

WHAT ARE THE HIGH PRAISES OF GOD?

Psalm 149

Let the high praises of God be in their mouth, and a two-edged sword in their hand; to execute vengeance upon the heathen. Verses 6-7a

When we enter into high praise, unsaved people come under conviction.

And punishment upon the people.
Verse 7b

Backslidden people are saved. People who are not living right and walking right will be convicted.

To bind their kings with chains and their nobles with fetters of iron.
Verse 8

Principalities and powers, the rulers of darkness of this world and spiritual wickedness in high places are bound.

To execute upon them the judgment written: this honour have all his saints. Praise yet the Lord.
Verse 9

When the Lord thy God shall bring thee into the land whither thou goest to possess it, and hath cast

WHAT ARE THE HIGH PRAISES OF GOD?

out many nations before thee, ... seven nations greater and mightier than thou; a And when the Lord thy God shall deliver them before thee; thou shalt smite them, and utterly destroy them; thou shalt make no covenant with them, nor shew mercy unto them.

Deuteronomy 7:1-2

We are to possess by driving out the previous tenants. In this way, we are to *"execute the judgment written."* This is an honor.

PRAISE AS WARFARE

O clap your hands, all ye people; shout unto God with the voice of triumph. For the LORD most high is terrible; he is a great King over all the earth. He shall subdue the people under us, and the nations under our feet. Psalm 47:1-3

Clapping is a sign of triumph and causes Jesus to rise up as a warring king.

PRAISE AS WARFARE

As Jesus made His triumphal entry into Jerusalem, great multitudes spread their garments before Him and praised Him crying out, *"Hosanna to the son of David: Blessed is he that cometh in the name of the Lord; Hosanna in the highest"* (Matthew 21:6).

This was the first account in the New Testament when Jesus allowed the people to praise Him. Consequently, we see Him rising up as a man of war, casting out all them that sold and bought in the Temple and overthrowing the tables of the money changers.

Out of the mouth of babes and sucklings hast thou ordained strength because of thine enemies, that thou mightest still the enemy and the avenger. Psalm 8:2

Praise stills the enemy.

And after these things I heard a great voice of much people in heaven, saying, Alleluia; Salvation, and glory, and honour, and power, unto the Lord our God.
Revelation 19:1

"Much people" were praising God.

And the four and twenty elders and the four beasts fell down and worshipped God that sat on the throne, saying, Amen; Alleluia.
Revelation 19:4

PRAISE AS WARFARE

The twenty-four elders the four beasts were all worshiping God.

And a voice came out of the throne, saying, Praise our God, all ye his servants, and ye that fear him, both small and great. Revelation 19:5

Now, all of God's servants were to praise Him.

And I heard as it were the voice of a great multitude, and as the voice of many waters, and as the voice of mighty thunderings, saying, Alleluia: for the Lord God omnipotent reigneth. Revelation 19:6

A great multitude was praising God.

MAKE A JOYFUL NOISE

And I fell at his feet to worship him. Revelation 19:10

John also worshiped God.

This is the second account of worship preceding war. Worship causes Jesus to rise as a mighty man of war.

And I saw heaven opened, and behold a white horse; and he that sat upon him was called Faithful and True, and in righteousness he doth judge and make war.
His eyes were as a flame of fire, and on his head were many crowns; and he had a name written, that no man knew, but he himself.

PRAISE AS WARFARE

And he was clothed with a vesture dipped in blood: and his name is called The Word of God.

And the armies which were in heaven followed him upon white horses, clothed in fine linen, white and clean.

And out of his mouth goeth a sharp sword, that with it he should smite the nations: and he shall rule them with a rod of iron: and he treadeth the winepress of the fierceness and wrath of Almighty God.

16 And he hath on his vesture and on his thigh a name written, King Of Kings, And Lord Of Lords.

Revelation 19:11-16

CLAPPING AS A POWERFUL FORM OF WARFARE

And he brought forth the king's son, and put the crown upon him, and gave him the testimony; and they made him king, and anointed him; and they clapped their hands, and said, God save the king. 2 Kings 11:12

This word *clapped* is translated from a Hebrew word that means "exultation, rejoicing, jubilation and triumph." We clap to celebrate Jesus.

CLAPPING AS A POWERFUL FORM OF WARFARE

All that pass by clap their hands at thee; they hiss and wag their head at the daughter of Jerusalem, saying, Is this the city that men call The perfection of beauty, The joy of the whole earth? Lamentations 2:15

This word *clap* was translated from the Hebrew word *sawfak*, which means "indignation, punishment, to vomit, and to smite." This passage speaks of the humiliation of the fallen Jerusalem.

Men shall clap their hands at him, and shall hiss him out of his place.
Job 27:23

This was Job's philosophy on the end of the wicked. This clapping was a form of punishment and indignation.

To hiss here meant "to whistle in scorn and derision."

There is no healing of thy bruise; thy wound is grievous: all that hear the bruit of thee shall clap the hands over thee: for upon whom hath not thy wickedness passed continually? Nahum 3:19

This word *clap* is translated from the Hebrew word *tawkah*, which means "to drive a nail or tent pin or a dart." When we clap, we humiliate the enemy, driving a nail into his plans. In this way, we execute the vengeance of our God and the judgment that has been written.

To Him who sits on the throne

And unto the Lamb

Be blessing

And glory

And honor

And power

Forever [1]

---
1. Lyrics by Don Moen

But the hour cometh, and now is, when the true worshippers shall worship the Father in spirit and in truth: for the Father seeketh such to worship him. John 4:23

WORSHIP LIKE THE ROYAL PRIESTHOOD YOU ARE

But ye are a chosen generation, a royal priesthood, an holy nation, a peculiar people; that ye should shew forth the praises of him who hath called you out of darkness into his marvellous light. 1 Peter 2:9

We must have the same dedication as the priest and Levites of the Old Testament. Even the musicians in that time, were to be as holy and sanctified as the priests. They were also courageous warriors, for when there was a battle, they went out before the rest of the troops, praising God in advance for victory.

STANDARDS FOR OUR WORSHIP

We must worship *"in spirit and in truth"* (see John 4:23)

To worship means "to pay homage or respect, to adore, to esteem, to magnify, to revere or to exalt." All of that is our desire.

Our worship must be the outpouring of our inner thoughts to God, the declaration of our love and commitment.

Coming to Him *"in truth"* means that we must display absolute openness and honestly before God, hiding nothing, exposing our entire life to the divine searchlight of the Holy Spirit.

Coming to Him *"in spirit"* means that our worship must include every part of our total human personality.

<u>1 Thessalonians 5:23</u>

A. The body, all five senses (our world-consciousness)

B. The soul, our intellect, emotions and will (our self-consciousness)

C. The spirit, the life of God in us (our God–consciousness)

STANDARDS FOR OUR WORSHIP

Worship is an active response to God whereby we declare His worth. It is not just a feeling; it is a declaration.

I. Declare His worth

    A. Because of who God is and what He does, we attribute to Him the glory that is due His name.

HIS WORTHINESS

Worthy is the Lamb that was slain

To receive power

And riches

And wisdom

And might

And honor

And glory

And blessing
>Revelation 5:12

II. Celebrate God

When we worship God, we celebrate Him, we extol Him, we boast in Him.

IN CONCLUSION

Worship is what Heaven is all about. In almost all scriptural references to Heaven, we are given the picture of the worthiness of God, of the glory due unto His name and of the joy to be found in His presence.

God has not reserved the pleasure of our being in His presence for eternity or for some later time. He has provided a means for us to come into His glorious presence while we are still here on this Earth.

Having therefore, brethren, boldness to enter into the holiest by the blood of Jesus, by a new and living way, which he hath consecrated for us, through the veil, that is to say, his flesh; and having an high priest over the house of God; let us draw near with a true heart in full assurance of faith, having our hearts sprinkled from an evil conscience, and our bodies washed with pure water. Hebrews 10:19-22

Worship is something that must happen when we know that we are in the presence of Almighty God. And, in order to worship, we must be in total alignment—body, soul and spirit—in agreement.

IN CONCLUSION

As noted previously, God did not design the Christian life to be lived under the domination of the soul, where emotions, intellect, and double-mindedness can rule. He desires that we discipline ourselves to be ruled by our spirit in an attitude of constant communion with Him, our Creator.

Psalm 98:1

O sing unto the Lord a new song. For he hath done marvellous things; his right hand, and his holy arm, hath gotten him the victory

Verse 4

Make a joyful noise unto the Lord, all the earth; make a loud noise, and rejoice, and sing praise.

Verse 5

Sing unto the Lord with the harp; with the harp, and the voice of a psalm.

Make a joyful noise unto the Lord, all ye lands.

Serve the Lord with gladness: come before his presence with singing.

Know ye that the Lord he is God: it is he that hath made us, and not we ourselves; we are his people, and the sheep of his pasture.

Enter into his gates with thanksgiving, and into his courts with praise: be thankful unto him, and bless his name.

For the Lord is good; his mercy is everlasting; and his truth endureth to all generations.

Psalm 100

Other Books by Prophetess Jackie Harewood

The Violent Take It by Force

Intercession Builds Bridges: Frequently Asked Questions About Intercession

Overshadowed by the Almighty

Ballistic Apostolic Prayer

Using Your Most Powerful Weapon

Warring with the Scriptures

The Violent Take it by Force

Intercession Made Easy

Jackie Harewood

Overshadowed by the Almighty

Understanding the Phenomenon Known as "Being Slain in the Spirit"

With a special chapter entitled
What Does God's Voice Sound Like?

Prophetess Jackie Harewood

Ballistic Apostolic Prayer

Jackie Harewood

Learning to Use Your Greatest Weapon

Prophetess Jackie Harewood

WARRING with the SCRIPTURES

Arm Yourself with Power-Packed Words to Reign in Victory

Prophetess Jackie Harewood

I Will Bless THEE

Discovering the Untapped Power of COVENANT

Apostle David Harewood

AUTHOR CONTACT PAGE

Prophetess Jackie Harewood
37041 Agnes Webb Avenue
Prairieville, LA 70769

(225) 772-4552

www.fcimbr.wordpress.com
www.iffcm.wordpress.com

jharewoodla@icloud.com

www.ingramcontent.com/pod-product-compliance
Lightning Source LLC
Chambersburg PA
CBHW031650040426
42453CB00006B/264